NEW YORK
FROM THE AIR

Featuring the photography of Neil Sutherland.
CLB 1430
This 1991 edition published by Crescent Books,
distributed by Outlet Book Company, Inc, a Random House Company,
225 Park Avenue South, New York, New York 10003.
© 1986 Colour Library Books Ltd, Godalming, Surrey, England.
All rights reserved.
Text filmsetting by Acesetters Ltd, Richmond, Surrey, England.
Printed and bound in Italy.
ISBN 0 517 49052 8
8 7 6 5 4 3 2

NEW YORK
FROM THE AIR

Text by
Bill Harris

CRESCENT BOOKS
NEW YORK

This book is fondly dedicated to the memory of A. Roy Knabenshue.

As he himself would probably modestly point out, what he did would eventually have been done by someone. Dozens of daring men had already done similar things.

What makes A. Roy Knabenshue of Toledo, Ohio, somebody special is what happened on Sunday afternoon, August 20, 1905. At precisely two o'clock in the afternoon, A. Roy became the first person ever to see New York from the air.

He had slipped into town several days before with his manager and a lot of odd-looking luggage. They went straight from the station to a vacant lot on West 62nd Street across from Central Park. They had previously contracted to have a ten-foot fence built around the space, and before anyone could ask too many questions, they disappeared behind it.

Though A. Roy stayed out of sight, his manager didn't. There were daily bulletins issued to eager reporters from behind the fence and thousands altered their evening strolling patterns in hopes of getting a glimpse of what was going on. Kids kept vigils of their own and police had their hands full keeping them from climbing the fence.

Finally A. Roy Knabenshue was ready to give them what they came to see. He had used his time to assemble a contraption he called "Toledo Number Two." (Number One, which he also had with him, didn't make it to the starting line.) His agent explained that Number Two could not be properly called an airship. It was, he said, "a dirigible balloon with air paddles."

It was a huge, hydrogen-filled gas bag with a trapeze-like structure suspended beneath it. When it rose from the vacant lot that Sunday afternoon, there was A. Roy in a crouched position smiling bravely at the huge crowd that had gathered in the park.

They had to crane their necks to see him. In no time at all A. Roy had reached his cruising altitude of one thousand feet – about the distance from the street to the beginning of the spear on top of the Chrysler Building.

Using his air paddles, he negotiated his dirigible balloon on a downtown course and did what every visitor from Toledo did in those days, he headed for Times Square.

By the time he got there, the crowd in the streets below had grown to more than 300,000 people. There was a lump in every throat as A. Roy Knabenshue sailed lazily over their heads.

A crowd of dignitaries assembled on the roof of the Times Tower waved as he went past, carefully noting that he was exactly twice as high from the street as they were. The wave was the aeronaut's signal to turn around and go back up to Central Park.

Before he disappeared again behind the wooden fence on West 62nd Street, he had been in the air one hour and 43 minutes and had covered a distance of almost exactly two miles.

The papers the next day described his adventure and reported that he had been able to see all the way downtown to the Statue of Liberty and by a simple turn of his head could see all the way up to Grant's Tomb. The city was even more impressed by what they had seen. Most of the major cities of Europe considered balloonists old stuff by the summer of '05. And A. Roy Knabenshue himself had already flown over the city of Toledo, Ohio. But New York had never seen anything like it.

Then he promised them that they hadn't seen anything yet. The next day people stayed home from work in anticipation, but A. Roy was in seclusion. No word was heard from him on

Tuesday, either. But finally, on Wednesday, his manager emerged to announce that the daring young man had been suffering from indigestion – described in some circles as butterflies in his stomach and gas pains in others – but that he was feeling fine again and ready for a second and more dramatic flight.

As he rose above the park for the second time it was quickly obvious that this trip would be different. For one thing, it was harder to see him up there. He had risen to a height of 5000 feet, nearly five times higher than the World Trade Center Observation Deck is today. And this time he went a mile further downtown, all the way to Madison Square and the Flatiron Building.

Why, you might ask, isn't his feat better remembered? By the time A. Roy Knabenshue came to New York, the world had turned its eye on a different form of flight. A couple of his fellow Ohioans were touring the world with a machine that could fly in spite of the fact that it was heavier than air. And Wilbur and Orville Wright were good promoters.

But that is not to say that balloonists weren't getting a lot of attention. On November 14, 1907, Thomas T. Lovelace boarded the German balloon *Pommern* in Philadelphia and sailed up the coast. When he reached Staten Island, he leaned out from the gondola and photographed soldiers inside the walls of Fort Wadsworth. A few days later, he boarded the battleship *U.S.S. Missouri* anchored in the harbor, photographs in hand. In his report to the Admiral of The Fleet he said "there will not be a standing army in any nation in the world in five to ten years." He also had photographs of the Admiral's flagship taken from the air, but neglected to point out the vulnerability they demonstrated.

By the time Mr. Lovelace flew from Philadelphia with a camera in his hand, the whole world was thrilled with the idea of aeronautics. In New York, daredevils were thrilling crowds with balloon ascents across the Hudson at Palisades Amusement Park and out in Coney Island. On Long Island, a half-dozen fields were turned into airports and the Manhattan Y.M.C.A. had established an adult education class in how to fly an airplane.

Yet no one had flown one of the newfangled machines over Manhattan. In the spring of 1909, in fact, the Wright Brothers stipulated in manufacturing contracts that anyone who paid the $7500 price of one of their flying machines had to sign a promise not to fly it over any cities. "The inventors fear that the falling of a man and an aerial automobile from the clouds into a crowded street might be somewhat disastrous for those who chanced to stop their progress," reported *The New York Times*.

But in October of the same year the rule was broken by no less a person than Wilbur Wright himself. The occasion was the Hudson-Fulton Fete, a week-long spectacle celebrating the 300th anniversary of the discovery of the river by Henry Hudson. There were parades all over town and an international naval review that brought the entire United States Atlantic Fleet together with the cream of navies from all over the world. Both Wilbur Wright and another aviation pioneer, Glenn Curtiss, shipped airplanes to a specially constructed field on Governor's Island and announced plans to participate in the festivities.

Unfortunately for both Mr. Curtiss and Mr. Wright, God seemed to have had other plans. It rained all week long. Though it didn't dampen anyone's enthusiasm nor cancel any torchlight parades, it wasn't what they call good flying weather. After 45 seconds in the air in an attempt to fly past the Statue of Liberty, Glenn Curtiss remembered a previous engagement and left town. Wilbur, on the other hand, decided to stick it out. Possibly the reason was that brother Orville was in Berlin and had that same week set a new altitude record of 1600 feet with Crown Prince Frederick William at his side shouting "higher! higher!"

Finally, the day after the Hudson-Fulton celebration ended, the weather cleared and, as if to preview the next 300 years, Wilbur Wright took off from Governor's Island and headed upriver. He was back 33 minutes and 33 seconds later after having flown over the British battleship H.M.S. *Drake*, anchored near Grant's Tomb. His average altitude was just 200 feet, but he didn't have the Kaiser egging him on.

Naturally, Wilbur Wright's performance set New York on fire, but the impact was softened by the fact that they had been celebrating the past for a week and didn't quite have room for the dessert of the future. They wouldn't get a real taste of that until nearly seven months later, when Glenn Curtiss came back to town. In an airplane.

All through the first decade of the 20th Century, anybody who wanted to get his name in the papers called in the press boys and announced that they were standing on the threshold of the age of flight. Often it was just as easy to get space by pooh-poohing the whole idea and pointing out that airplanes were no more than motorized box kites that would never amount to anything more than a novelty.

When John Jacob Astor opened his fancy hotel at Times Square in 1904, he announced that the roof had been designed for easy conversion to a landing space for airships and every new hotel in town made the same claim.

But until Glenn Curtiss flew into town on May 29, 1910, nobody seriously believed that the airplane had a future as a carrier of passengers, mail or freight.

Curtiss had left Albany that morning at 7:03 and arrived at Governor's Island at noon. He collected a $10,000 prize from *The New York World* for his trouble. But more significantly, his little biplane came down the Hudson at an average speed of 54 miles an hour. The fastest train in service at the time was the New York Central's Twentieth Century Limited, whose top speed was 49.6 miles an hour. The handwriting was on the wall.

Even more significant to the future of commercial aviation than distance or speed was the route Curtiss flew. Until that point every other long-distance flight had been planned over flat terrain with no trees, houses or sudden updrafts. Curtiss flew over high cliffs and mountains, deep canyons and varying air currents. He had built a heavier than normal engine to help him over the mountains and he added heavy metal caissons and a series of airbags in case he should drop into the river. His gas tank was double the normal size and the plane itself was the smallest used by anyone up to that point for a long-distance attempt.

In spite of the extra gasoline capacity, he was forced to land near Poughkeepsie for nearly an hour to pick up more fuel. In some of the spots where updrafts were heavy, he pumped more oil into the engine to help it handle the strain. As he flew over

the Storm King Mountain, he was using so much oil that the blue haze behind him gave rise to rumors that he had gone down.

The oil problem forced him to land again for another hour at a farm near 214th Street and Broadway where, by the rules of the game, since he was within the city limits, he could have claimed his cash prize. But he wasn't in it for the money, he said, and took off again for the last leg of the trip down Manhattan's West Side.

New Yorkers were irritated with Curtiss for having left town the year before, and going on was probably the smartest thing he did. After he took off from Poughkeepsie and word came that he was on his way, every trans-Hudson ferryboat was filled to capacity and people were just riding back and forth. There were six super ocean liners in port, including the *Mauretania*, and all of them turned off their engines so they could hear Curtiss's eight cylinders as he approached. When he did, they blew long whistle blasts in salute.

He arrived at Governor's Island to a hero's welcome, but like the vessels in the river, all was silence until they heard him coming. It was the sound that made this type of aircraft something special. An officer at Governor's Island said it was "a harsh noise, halfway between a rattle and a whir, only comparable to a trout reel badly in need of oiling."

But it was music to everyone's ears. The age of flight had finally arrived in New York. And, more important to him, New York had finally forgiven Mr. Curtiss for having run out on their celebration the previous fall.

He was about to run out on them again. "My machine in the aerodrome is ready to turn about and duplicate the trip," he said. But instead he opted to go back upstate that afternoon by train. "I'm experimenting with a craft designed to start up from the water as well as alight on it," he explained. "I already can alight all right, but part of the blade is under water and that prevents me from starting up again." A thing like that can worry a man. New York knew he had to go. New York knew just as well he'd eventually figure it all out.

Though their faith in Glenn Curtiss and the future of commercial aviation was restored that day in

1905, the City of New York waited until 1931 to open what passed for a municipal airport. The City of Newark, New Jersey had opened a facility of 68 acres of reclaimed swamp in 1928, but Mayor Jimmy Walker thought he had the key to taking away their claims of being the world's busiest airport. The site New York had picked was a peninsula in East Brooklyn jutting out into Jamaica Bay. Glenn Curtiss had long since figured out how to start up an airplane from the water without getting wet and the future of long distance aviation at that point seemed clearly tied to airports with access to long stretches of water.

But in this case long distance proved an insurmountable problem. Though the field they named for Floyd Bennett, the pilot who took Admiral Byrd across the North Pole in 1926, had lots of open water around it and a 220-foot ramp for handling seaplanes, passengers considered it too far from Manhattan and took their business elsewhere.

In 1939, "elsewhere" was more than likely to be North Beach Airport in the Jackson Heights section of Queens. The W.P.A. project that reclaimed the wetlands at the edge of the East River's Flushing Bay cost the taxpayers $22 million and seemed worth every penny, because the advertised travel time to the edge of the runway from the edge of Times Square was just 22 minutes.

The name "North Beach" vanished into history very quickly when the airport was renamed in honor of Mayor Fiorello LaGuardia. The 22-minute trip from Times Square has vanished into history, too. But a reminder of the airport's beginnings is its Marine Terminal, which was built to handle transatlantic air travel using seaplanes. The day it opened it had six airline tenants including Air France and Lufthansa and, of course, Pan Am.

Meanwhile, out in Southeast Queens, people were writing letters to the Borough President complaining about the pollution that was ruining swimming at Idlewild Point in Jamaica Bay. The city's response was to close the beach and turn the point into a golf course. It wasn't until 1942, when everyone agreed that water-based planes would soon be replaced by aircraft that needed plenty of runway space, that the City decided it needed a big international airport if it was going to survive as a major destination. They began by moving little communities and filling in the marshes around the golf course. It took from April, 1942 until July, 1948 to create the nearly 5,000 acres that became New York International Airport. Folks who used to swim or play golf there went right on calling it "Idlewild" and the rest of us followed their lead. The airport got an official name everyone would use when it was rededicated as John F. Kennedy International Airport on December 24, 1963.

One of the glide paths into Kennedy goes right past Floyd Bennett Field, which is a half-dozen miles closer to Manhattan. But there are no big signs that say "if the airport were here, you'd be on the ground now." If the international airport had been placed there, that whole section of Brooklyn would probably have disappeared into it. J.F.K. serves 15 U.S. flag carriers, 47 foreign carriers, 14 supplemental airlines and nine commuter airlines. And that's just for passengers. Eighteen carriers use the airport for cargo only. In addition to nine separate passenger terminal buildings, there are 31 cargo-handling buildings and fourteen aircraft hangars, not counting Pan Am's engine overhaul building and a fuel storage section that holds 32 million gallons of aircraft fuel. It's all served by 32 miles of highways, nine miles of runways and 25 miles of taxiways.

And that's just J.F.K! Newark and LaGuardia Airports are every bit as busy. The three airports together handle more than 75 million passengers a year. Well over 60 percent of all transatlantic air travel is to and from New York. About ten percent of all domestic travel is through the same facilities. A total of 104 airlines serve New York and some 1.6 million tons of cargo are handled here every year.

But it's a story that goes beyond numbers. Though not all 75 million people who fly in and out of New York get a clear view of the city from the air, those who do don't forget the experience any time soon. Even people who come and go on a regular basis can't resist taking a peek out the window when the seat belt sign goes on and the flight attendant orders everyone to extinguish all smoking materials.

The view out there is New York from the air. There is no experience like it anywhere even if you see it every day.

13

45

65

Picture Captions

Page 9

For several years after the Statue of Liberty was dedicated by President Grover Cleveland, people knew it as "Bartholdi's statue," honoring its sculptor Frederic Auguste Bartholdi. Her official name is "Liberty Enlightening the World." In our enlightened times, people have taken to calling her "the lady." And why not? She's 11,812 inches tall and every inch a lady.

Pages 10 and 11

The star-shaped structure below the Statue of Liberty's pedestal is Fort Wood, built in 1808 as part of the defenses of New York. Another fort, Castle Williams, is across the Bay on Governor's Island. Its mate is Castle Clinton over in Battery Park. None of them ever fired a shot in anger.

Pages 12 and 13

The Queensboro Bridge, also known as the 59th Street Bridge, crosses Roosevelt Island on its way from Long Island City to the heart of Manhattan. The 7,450-foot cantilever bridge was designed in 1909 by Gustav Lindenthal. Before the overhead Roosevelt Island Tramway was built between the island and Manhattan in 1976, access from the bridge to what had been known as Welfare Island was by an elevator in the building with the tall smokestacks.

Pages 14 and 15

The reservoir in Central Park covers 106 acres of former meadowland. It once had a mate, which was drained in 1920 to create the Great Lawn behind the Metropolitan Museum of Art.

Pages 16 and 17

The twin-spired building in the center is the Waldorf-Astoria Hotel, which moved uptown from the present site of the Empire State Building in 1931, the same year the National Broadcasting Company moved into the building with the Art Deco spiked crown. N.B.C. and its parent, Radio Corporation of America, moved again two years later into Rockefeller Center's R.C.A. Building two blocks away. Their former building on Lexington Avenue at 51st Street has been known as the General Electric Building ever since.

Pages 18 and 19

The first Dutch settler along this stretch of the East River south of 49th Street named his farm "Turtle Bay." The name is still used for the neighborhood dominated by the buildings of the United Nations. Before the 544-foot Secretariat was built in 1950, the neighborhood was a sorry collection of rotting piers, slaughterhouses and breweries. The land for the U.N. site was bought with an $8.5 million gift from John D. Rockefeller, Jr.

Pages 20 and 21

The lift bridge of the Triborough Bridge that connects Manhattan with the South Bronx was designed in 1936 by Othmar H. Ammann, who gave us the George Washington Bridge five years earlier. In the 1920s he designed the three bridges that connect Staten Island with New Jersey. After designing the Bronx-Whitestone and Throgs Neck bridges, he went back to Staten Island to do the Verrazano-Narrows Bridge in 1961.

Pages 22 and 23

Shea Stadium, overlooking the Jackson Heights section of Queens, was built in 1964 as a home for the New York Mets. The infield seating was designed to rotate to make it useful as a football stadium as well a place to watch baseball. Unfortunately, the people who regard football as big business took their business elsewhere. It was good enough, on the other hand, for the Beatles in 1965 and for Pope John Paul II in 1979.

Pages 24 and 25

From this angle you can tell who is really working late in the W.R. Grace Building on 42nd Street near Sixth Avenue, in front of the Empire State Building, or in the New York Telephone Building to its right and across Sixth Avenue.

Pages 26 and 27

The four-masted bark *Peking*, built in Hamburg, Germany, in 1911, is one of the last commercial sailing vessels ever built. The iron-hulled *Wavertree* across the slip at South Street Seaport was built in 1885 in England and saw service between there and India. In the days before iron-hulled ships called at the Port of New York, the major port activity was on the East River, where fast currents kept it ice-free in the winter.

Pages 28 and 29

It only lasts for about 15 minutes and it doesn't happen every day. But seeing a sunset from Brooklyn with Manhattan basking in its glory is one of the most wonderful things about New York. And the best part is that, like snowflakes, no two sunsets are exactly alike.

Pages 30 and 31

So it's not the tallest building in the world. So what? The Empire State Building is still one of the most beautiful. Credit for that goes to William F. Lamb, of the architectural firm Shreve, Lamb and Harmon, who designed it in 1931. The budget for building it was $60 million. The actual cost was below $50 million. And look what we got for their money!

Pages 32 and 33

The site of the 1964-65 World's Fair was a huge dump before it became Flushing Meadows and the setting for the "World of Tomorrow" at the 1939 Fair. The symbol of that Fair, the Trylon and Perisphere, stood on the same spot as the stainless steel Unisphere. Grand Central Parkway, which cuts the park in half, was built across the dump in 1932.

Pages 34 and 35

This is similar to one of the views from the top of the World Trade Center. Washington Square Arch, in the heart of Greenwich Village, is a little left of center. The wide avenue a little right of center is Broadway. The neighborhood in the foreground on the left is SoHo.

Page 36

Central Park extends 2.5 miles from 59th Street to this stretch of 110th Street from Central Park West, an extension of Eighth Avenue, east to Fifth Avenue. All of the Park's entrances were given names by the designers Frederick Law Olmstead and Calvert Vaux. They named this one at the northwest corner the "Stranger's Gate."

Page 37

The Civic Center begins here with the gold pyramid on top of the United States Court House, designed by Cass Gilbert in 1936. It rises above Saint Andrew's Roman Catholic Church and the new Police Headquarters. Adolph Weinman's 25-foot statue *Civic Fame* stands on top of McKim, Mead and White's 1914 Municipal Building, which houses most city government offices. City Hall itself, designed in 1802 by John McComb and Joseph Mangin, is the wedding cake of a building in the center of the park. The building behind it is the infamous Tweed Courthouse built in 1872, paying a profit of some $12 million for the boss of Tammany Hall. Crowning the row of buildings across Broadway from the park is Cass Gilbert's 1913 masterpiece, the Gothic tower of the Woolworth Building.

Pages 38 and 39

Any booster will tell you that land in the New York area is the most valuable real estate in the world. But this parcel that separates Route 22 and the New Jersey Turnpike Extension serving Newark Airport seems to have been overlooked, even though it could easily support a small, suburban housing development. It could be that it is too noisy there. The white building on the right is the airport's North Terminal, home of People Express. The low-priced airline accounts for some 40 percent of the air traffic in and out of Newark.

Pages 40 and 41

Construction in the area around Citicorp Center at Lexington Avenue and 54th Street hasn't stopped since its slant-roofed tower was finished in 1978. Though architects don't appear to have much more in mind than making flat-topped boxes with monotonous rows of windows, Philip Johnson and John Burgee made them all sit up and take notice with the broken pediment on top of their A.T.&T. Building over on Madison Avenue and 55th Street. But from the look of some of the unfinished buildings nearby, the winds of change aren't blowing too hard yet.

Pages 42 and 43

One of the tales they tell about Mayor Fiorello LaGuardia is that he refused to get off an airplane that brought him here to Newark Airport. "I bought a ticket to New York," Hizzhonor is reported to have said. But between 1928 and 1939, Newark Airport was the only game in town. When it first opened, it was served by just one airline, which was called the Colonial Company. They still fly there, under the name American Airlines. United Airlines, whose plane is in the foreground, began service to Newark in 1929 under the name National Air Transport.

Page 44

The Ambrose lightship, one of the star attractions at South Street Seaport, formerly saw service as the beacon at the end of Ambrose Channel, the entrance to New York harbor. The vessel is named for John Wolfe Ambrose, the engineer who designed the channel in the 1890s.

Page 45

The large building with the gray roof at the corner of Park Avenue and 66th Street is the Seventh Regiment Armory. The roof covers a huge drill hall, 187 by 290 feet. The interior was designed by Louis Comfort Tiffany, who hired a young up-and-coming architect named Stanford White to help him with the elaborate Victorian details in stained glass and bronze.

Pages 46 and 47

Goldwater Memorial Hospital, on Roosevelt Island to the left of the Queensboro Bridge, was designed with short wings so the chronically ill patients there could enjoy views of the East River. The Tramway, built in 1976, serves tenants in the apartment buildings to the right of the bridge.

Pages 48 and 49

The barrel-roofed building in the foreground is the 69th Regiment Armory, the site of the 1913 "Armory Show," which introduced cubist painting to America. The complex of white buildings with the clock tower is the home of the Metropolitan Life Insurance Company. The building topped with a gold pyramid is the New York Life Insurance Company, built on the site of the original Madison Square Garden. The bronze wall between them is the Merchandise Mart, whose perpetrators destroyed the former Jerome Mansion, the only designated landmark ever to be torn down.

Pages 50 and 51

Think the Yanks'll take the pennant? If they do, they'll fill all 54,028 seats here in Yankee Stadium. Though it's called "the house that Ruth built," Babe Ruth wouldn't know the place. It was "improved" in 1976 at a cost of $100 million. In 1979, the taxpayers were asked to cough up another $1 million to correct some of the improvements. Was it worth it? Sure, if the Yanks take the pennant.

Pages 52 and 53

When John D. Rockefeller, Jr. had his office in the R.C.A. Building, this was the view he had from the window. It has been altered somewhat since his day, of course. The crown-topped box on the right has replaced the Astor Hotel in Times Square, and the old Times Tower looked like the lighted image of it painted on the facade of a building at Broadway and 42nd Street. The other lighted building (center of picture), with the mansard roof, is the former Knickerbocker Hotel, once the home of Enrico Caruso.

Page 54

The building on the far right at the water's edge is the terminal of the Staten Island Ferry. Two of the boats in service are licensed to carry 6,000 passengers, the largest such certificates in the world. The round trip between Battery Park and St. George, Staten Island is still a bargain at 25 cents.

Page 55

In an earlier time of movie-making, directors used the Queensboro Bridge as a backdrop looking out from Manhattan Terraces and apartment windows to let you know that the characters inside were people of some substance. The view of the bridge from the Sutton Place neighborhood on the East River is still romantic and it still spells success. But as everyone knows, they don't make movies like they used to.

Pages 56 and 57

Looking from east to west across the middle of Central Park, the ever-expanding Metropolitan Museum of Art seems about to enfold Cleopatra's Needle behind it at 81st Street. The Museum of Natural History at the edge of the park on the other side may meet the Metropolitan coming across the great lawn one day.

Pages 58 and 59

Lower Manhattan, from Castle Clinton up the East River to the Brooklyn Bridge, has changed hundreds of times since the Dutch built a fort on the site of the green-roofed Custom House at the edge of Battery Park in 1626. But from the day the Stock Market crashed in 1929 until 1960, when the Chase Manhattan Bank built its 60-story tower, no riveters' guns were heard south of City Hall. They've been making up for lost time ever since.

Pages 60 and 61

Meadow Lake, in the center of Flushing Meadows-Corona Park, was the site of Billy Rose's Aquacade in the 1939 World's Fair. The lake is still there, as are a few of the buildings built for the Fair's 1964 successor, but now it is surrounded by highways: Grand Central Parkway on the left, Van Wyck Expressway on the right, the Long Island Expressway behind the Aquacade, and Jewell Avenue in the foreground. Mount Hebron Cemetery is to the right of Van Wyck Expressway.

Page 62 top

Governor's Island was the site of the first Dutch settlement while Peter Minuit was saving up to buy the bigger Manhattan Island from the Indians. Today it is headquarters of the United States Coast Guard, with responsibility for the entire Eastern Seaboard and inland waters as far west as the Continental Divide. It's a terrific place to live, but you have to join the Coast Guard first. The island is off limits to the general public.

Page 62 bottom

During the period of restoration, the Statue of Liberty was all but hidden from view behind what the Guinness Book of Records says is the largest construction scaffold ever built. Liberty's new torch was crafted in the long, silver shed at her feet by French artisans.

Page 63

The red-roofed buildings in the foreground on Ellis Island were once hospital and dormitory facilities. Some 20 percent of the 12 million immigrants who passed through the reception center on the other side of the ferry slip were held here before being admitted into the United States. Less than two percent were ultimately refused entry.

Pages 64 and 65

Vehicles coming into Manhattan from New Jersey through the Lincoln Tunnel can avoid using Manhattan streets by the system of ramps that takes buses into the Port Authority Bus Terminal. The ramps also serve a parking garage on the roof. The Jacob K. Javits Convention Center, the glass structure on the extreme left, is a new arrival in this Hell's Kitchen neighborhood.

Pages 66 and 67

When Colonel Jacob Rupert, owner of the New York Yankees, built this stadium in the Mott Haven section of the West Bronx, it was the largest stadium in the world, with a capacity of 75,000. That was in 1922. Today it can hold a handful more than 54,000. The original price was $3 million. It cost $100 million to make it more comfortable.

Pages 68 and 69

Home to thousands of ultra-orthodox Jewish Hasidim, the Brooklyn neighborhood of Williamsburg, between the Manhattan Bridge on the left and the Williamsburg Bridge on the right, includes the site of the Brooklyn Navy Yard and the only electrical generating plant in the borough.

Pages 70 and 71

When Mayor LaGuardia moved there in 1940, Gracie Mansion became the only official mayor's residence in any city in the United States. It is also the only remaining still-inhabited country house in New York City. It was built by Archibald Gracie, a New York merchant, in 1799 on the foundations of a house that had been destroyed by British ships in the East River in 1776. Carl Schurz Park, behind the house on the edge of the Manhattan neighborhood of Yorkville, is named for a German immigrant who was a United States Senator and editor of the *New York Post*. The pathway over the F.D.R. Drive is John Finley Walk, named for an editor of *The New York Times* who enjoyed nothing more than walking the 32-mile circuit of Manhattan Island.

Page 72 top

There are 508 miles of waterfront in the five boroughs of New York City, but very few restaurants with water views. The Water Club, which floats in the East River at the end of 30th Street, is one of the exceptions.

Page 72 bottom

Further uptown at 39th Street, the Franklin D. Roosevelt Drive passes a Con Edison electric generating plant. The tall structure to the left of it is an apartment house that is a harbinger of the change arriving at the edge of this formerly industrial neighborhood known as Murray Hill.

Page 73

The lift bridge span of the Triborough Bridge, between Randall's Island and 125th Street in Manhattan, dwarfs the Willis Avenue Bridge just upriver and the shorter Third Avenue Bridge above it. The blue lift bridge above them carries trains of the Metro North commuter lines from Westchester and Connecticut over to Park Avenue and down toward Grand Central Terminal.

Pages 74 and 75

The New Englanders who came to City Island with a dream of a seaport competing with New York, incorporated the 230-acre island as part of Westchester County. Their descendants saw the error of their ways and became part of The Bronx, and New York City, in 1895.

Pages 76 and 77

In the early days of aviation, pilots found their way from one city to another by following the railroad tracks connecting them. The first person to fly from New York to Philadelphia followed this route of the Pennsylvania Railroad. He dropped green rubber balls along the way to announce his presence. The railroad is now called Amtrak, the highway next to it is the New Jersey Turnpike and the wetlands they cross are now known as "meadowlands."

Pages 78 and 79

Pier 17, part of South Street Seaport between the East River and the Fulton Fish Market, provides one of the best spots in New York for sitting and watching the world go by. The two boats at the end of Pier 16, the sailing schooner *Pioneer* and the sidewheeler *Andrew Fletcher*, take passengers out into the wonderful world that is New York harbor.

Pages 80 and 81

New England? Of course not, it's The Bronx. It is City Island in Eastchester Bay. Back in the 18th century, people who lived there had dreams of building a seaport that would take most of the business away from the port of New York. Fortunately, their plan failed and life on City Island hasn't changed much since.

Pages 82 and 83

Just north of the Queens side of the Queensboro Bridge is the Ravenswood power plant, operated by Con Edison. The huge electric generator inside, which was a little temperamental when it was first installed, is known to its neighbors who muddled through the break-in period as "Big Allis," for its builder, the Allis Chalmers Company

Page 84

Greenery checkers the gleaming steps of the Trump Tower, a smart combination of offices and shops on Fifth Avenue.

Page 85

Going down Fifth Avenue from Grand Army Plaza, flanked by The Plaza Hotel and the tall, white General Motors Building, the scene includes the Crown Building and Tiffany's, facing each other on the corner of 57th Street. In the little more than a half-mile down to 42nd Street are the best retail and office addresses in the world.

Pages 86 and 87

In 1931, a young bandleader named Ozzie Nelson took his band up to New Rochelle to play a date at Glen Island Casino. The music was broadcast on WOR radio "live from the water's edge on Long Island Sound." The broadcast series lasted well into the 1940s, featuring such big bands as Glen Gray, Claude Thornhill, the Dorsey Brothers and, of course, Glenn Miller, who recorded "In The Mood" in that white building on the island's northeast tip. As many as 1400 people a night made the trip across the bridge to listen and lindy for a $1.50 cover charge.

Pages 88 and 89

The structure that looks like a base drum lying on its side is Madison Square Garden. The large building to the left of it is the General Post Office on Eighth Avenue at 33rd Street. The inscription above the columns on the front is one of the most famous in the world: "Neither snow nor rain nor heat..." You know the rest. As if to back up the inscription, the building is open 365 days a year, 24 hours a day.

Pages 90 and 91

If you make a wrong turn coming from New York through the Lincoln Tunnel and inadvertently get on to the New Jersey Turnpike heading south, the next exit is at Newark, about 15 minutes down the road. Though it doesn't seem so from this angle, it is the largest city in New Jersey and one of the 50 largest cities in the United States.

Pages 92 and 93

The Queens County Jockey Club is better known as Aqueduct Race Track, or the "Big A" to its intimates. Its history dates back to 1894; its name comes from a long-gone aqueduct that ran next to it carrying water to the independent City of Brooklyn from its chain of reservoirs further out on Long Island.

Pages 94 and 95

If you asked a cab driver to take you to John Jay Park, you should be taken here to this spot of green next to the F.D.R. Drive at 77th Street. But the driver might be taken aback if you asked for Cherokee Place. It's the street that runs along the inland side of the park, named for one of the clubhouses of Tammany Hall that used to get out the vote in this Upper East Side neighborhood.

Page 96

When the Roman Catholic Church acquired the block on Fifth Avenue at 50th Street in 1810, one of the plans was to turn it into a cemetery. They had a perfectly good cathedral down on Mulberry Street... it's still there, in fact. But nearly 50 years later they decided to join the march uptown and hired James Renwick Jr. to design this new Saint Patrick's, which was dedicated in 1879 by America's first Cardinal, John McCloskey.

Page 97

Looking west from the Chrysler Building is the open space above Grand Central Terminal and the Chanin Building across 42nd Street from it. The white building with the black vertical stripes is the headquarters of New York Telephone on Sixth Avenue across from Bryant Park. Between it and the crown-topped Astor Plaza in Times Square is the U.S.S. *Intrepid* moored on the Hudson River.

Pages 98 and 99

The lighting on the Empire State Building and the Metropolitan Life tower to its left was the work of Douglas Leigh, who earned a reputation in New York in the 1940s with electric signs he called "spectaculars" in Times Square. The spectacle included a block-long waterfall and a cigarette smoker who blew 20-foot smoke rings out into the street.

Pages 100 and 101

From the time the first settlers arrived here in the 1650s, this Queens neighborhood was known as "Whitepot." In the early part of this century, a real estate developer created a community of Tudor and Colonial houses and apartments. They surrounded them with gardens and changed the name Whitepot to Forest Hills to dramatize its nearness to Forest Park. The charm lives on in the vicinity of the West Side Tennis Club on the south side of the Long Island Railroad tracks.

Pages 102 and 103

Pier A, on the edge of Battery Park, is the base of a little red fireboat and is one of the oldest fire stations still active in the United States. The stadium-like structure in the park is Castle Clinton, and the flagpole at the end of the plaza in front of it marks the spot where it is said Peter Minuit bought Manhattan for $24, back in 1626. If that's true, he got his feet wet. The river bank was a few yards further inland back then.

Pages 104 and 105

The Bronx-Whitestone Bridge gets half of its name from this Queens community of Whitestone. The neck of land beyond the bridge is known as College Point. Beyond that is Rikers Island, officially part of The Bronx, but connected to Queens by a bridge near LaGuardia Airport.

Pages 106 and 107

The highway interchange on the right is the approach to the Brooklyn Bridge at City Hall Park. The Civic Center is above it, the Financial District below. When City Hall was built, its north facade was faced with rough stone because it was thought no one would ever go around to that side. From this angle it's obvious they were wrong.

Pages 108 and 109

Only memories remain in Flushing Meadows Park of the wonderful New York World's Fair of 1964-65. The large building in the center is a holdover from the Fair of 1939-40. It was the New York City Building then, now it's the Queens Museum, containing a constantly-updated model of New York City. The airy globe behind it is the symbol of the 64-65 Fair, U.S. Steel's Unisphere. The ruin in the foreground is what is left of Philip Johnson's New York State Pavilion. The "T"-shaped structure across Grand Central Parkway is the 64-65 Transportation Pavilion, now a restaurant.

Pages 110 and 111

Roosevelt Island is two-and-a-half miles from one end to the other. It sits 300 yards away from Manhattan in the East River, but, to the 5,500 people who live there, it is an oasis that could be 300 miles from the city. Fortunately it isn't. The trip by Tram to 59th Street and Second Avenue takes 3.5 minutes.

Pages 112 and 113

When South Street Seaport was "restored," hungry real estate developers considered it their sacred duty to create a wall of buildings around it. They were in such a hurry that when the wreckage of a 19th century sailing ship was found in a foundation excavation, it was quickly covered up so the construction schedule wouldn't be delayed.

Pages 114 and 115

What could be more beautiful than the nighttime view from the top of the Empire State Building, especially when the Metropolitan Life tower is decked out in colored lights and the Con Edison tower behind it echoes the feeling of celebration? The "V"-shaped swath of light in the foreground is Broadway meeting Fifth Avenue at Madison Square in front of the Flatiron Building.

Pages 116 and 117

Queens Boulevard winds its way through Forest Hills and Rego Park on its way to the Queensboro Bridge. The name for Forest Hills was chosen to reflect the rural qualities that have long since been crowded out by high rise apartments. Rego Park gets its name from the developers who built it, the Real Good Construction Company.

Pages 118 and 119

One of the nice things about a visit to the Empire State Building Observatories is getting the feeling that you could reach out and touch the buildings of Rockefeller Center just uptown, or toss a Frisbee into Central Park not far beyond. This view of midtown, looking north and west, has the added advantage of including the Empire State Building itself.

Page 120

Brooklyn Heights has been a fashionable place to live since the Dutch began the move to the suburbs in the 17th century. As is typical of New York, the oldest buildings there were built around the time of the Civil War. The neighborhood became frozen in time when it was designated a historic district in 1965. The piers that block its view of Manhattan are, mercifully, not included in the historic preservation.

Page 121

The greatest diorama ever created by man... It's even more impressive when you think it all started with a $24 investment.

Pages 122 and 123

The Bedford-Stuyvesant neighborhood in Brooklyn is New York's largest black community. In the 18th century, when the city was named Breuckelen and this neighborhood was open farmland, about a quarter of the population was made up of black slaves owned by Dutch farmers.

Pages 124 and 125

People who live in the apartment buildings on Roosevelt Island are technically Manhattanites. In 1973, two years before the apartments were opened, the island's name was changed from Welfare Island in an attempt to upgrade its image. It had been given that name in 1921 for the same reason. Prior to that it had been called Blackwell's Island and was known for a hundred years as the site of a workhouse, a lunatic asylum and one of the meanest prisons the city has ever seen. The Dutch, who were here first, called it Hog Island.

Pages 126 and 127

College Point in Queens has an enviable position between the runways of Flushing Airport and LaGuardia Airport. But if it's noisy, it's also handy to transportation.

Pages 128 and 129

The buildings of the United Nations are on the edge of New York and the institution itself is very important to the city. But these landscaped acres are technically outside the jurisdiction of both the city and federal governments. The tall building, opened in 1950, is the Secretariat; to the right of it is the General Assembly Building, built in 1952. The building on the left, facing 42nd Street, is the Dag Hammarskjold Library, built in 1963.

Pages 130 and 131

Improving the breed north of New York City is largely an after-hours activity conducted by thousands of fans who come out for the evening trotting races at Yonkers Raceway.

Pages 132 and 133

The body of water dancing in the sun is Harlem Meer, at the northeast corner of Central Park. Like so many of the park's features, the Meer is man-made. It was created in 1866 by flooding a meadow. The circular structure is the Louela D. Lasker Pool, which becomes an ice skating rink in the winter months. The formal Conservatory Garden is at the other end of the Meer at East 105th Street.

Pages 134 and 135

City Island Avenue, which runs down the length of the island, turns around and runs back again, is a wonderful place for a leisurely stroll, some window shopping and an occasional stop for some of the best seafood anywhere in New York.

Pages 136 and 137

Many buildings on the New York skyline are lighted at night, but the bright idea started with the Empire State Building. The lighting scheme changes to mark special occasions. The most special of all is March 17, when the tower is bathed in green, a tribute to all Irish New Yorkers, but especially the building's first President, Governor Al Smith.

Pages 138 and 139

The bridge to carless Roosevelt Island serves the garage they call "Motorgate." It also gives access for the Department of Sanitation, whose trucks go to the next building on the right, called the AVAC Building. Garbage from all the apartments on the island is sent to AVAC through a system of underground vacuum tubes to be shredded, compacted and packed in sealed containers.

Page 140

The Chanin Building, diagonally across the intersection of Lexington Avenue and 42nd Street from the Chrysler tower, was built in 1929, the year before William Van Alen built the Art Deco building across the street. It was designed by the firm of Sloan and Robertson, whose client was Irwin Chanin, an architect himself. But Chanin was also a developer, and though his building is one hundred feet shorter than the Woolworth Building, it has more floors and more rentable space.

Page 141

Foley Square, the address of the pyramid-topped Federal Courthouse and the hexagonal New York County Courthouse, is the former site of Five Points, which was in the 18th and early 19th centuries the roughest neighborhood in the city. Though it was considered safe after a cleanup in 1852, it produced a young Al Capone a half-century later. The square is named for Thomas Foley, a local saloon keeper and Tammany politician who died the same year Scarface Al left for Chicago.

Pages 142 and 143

Visitors to the Empire State Building Observatories can't help noticing the tall brick structure to the east of it on 34th Street and Park Avenue, especially at night when its top is accented with orange light. It's an office building developed by the city over the top of Norman Thomas High School. The black tower on the other side of the Empire State Building is also on 34th Street; it is Penn Plaza, one of the buildings above Penn Station.

Pages 144 and 145

Going north on the Hudson River past such cities as Yonkers, you can't help wondering what Henry Hudson would say if he could see it now. But on the west side, except for an occasional tall structure like the telephone transmission tower in the distance, the landscape of the Palisades hasn't changed much. Don't be fooled! There are millions of people living over there among the trees in New Jersey's Bergen County.

Pages 146 and 147

Citicorp Center, on Lexington Avenue at 54th Street, raised its slanted roof on the skyline in 1978. The rakish angle was intended to be a platform for a solar energy collector, an idea that was abandoned before it saw the light of day. The apartment buildings along the shore of the East River are in the neighborhood called Sutton Place and are home to the rich and famous who long ago established this as the best address in town.

Pages 148 and 149

If the streets of New York were really paved with gold, the heaviest concentration would surely be in the Financial District south from the World Trade Center and World Financial Center to Battery Park. But if the only visible gold is made by the setting sun, visitors who make advance reservations can look at billions of dollars worth of gold in the five levels of vaults under the Federal Reserve Bank near the twin towers.

Pages 150 and 151

The group of apartment buildings on the other side of the Macombs Dam Bridge leading from Yankee Stadium stands on Coogan's Bluff, the site of the former Polo Grounds where the New York Giants once played baseball. The bridge across the Harlem River in the foreground is the 145th Street Bridge.

Pages 152 and 153

A narrow stretch of Forest Hills is tucked between Queens Boulevard on the left and Grand Central Parkway on the right. The view across the Parkway is of Willow Lake, at the south end of Flushing Meadows-Corona Park.

Pages 154 and 155

Pace University, overlooking the Civic Center and the Brooklyn Bridge approaches, was originally a school of accounting, but now offers programs ranging from business to the arts. It faces Park Row, once the center of newspaper publishing.

Pages 156 and 157

Many of the Dutch who settled Nieuw Amsterdam did the same thing people have been doing ever since; they moved to the suburbs. There are towns all the way up the Hudson as far as Albany that trace their ancestry back to Dutch farmers. This one, Yonkers, gets its name from the Dutch word for noblemen, *De Jonkers.*

Pages 158 and 159

As any Jerseyan will tell you, Liberty Island is closer to New Jersey than it is to New York. The Garden State provides a busy backdrop for the lady in the harbor. It also gives her some exciting sunsets, even though she is facing the other way.

Pages 160 and 161

The Annenburg Building of Mount Sinai Hospital at 100th Street overlooking Central Park does its best to dominate the Fifth Avenue skyline. It owes its color to a coating of rust on its steel curtain wall. That was intentional, of course, but certainly not for aesthetic reasons. The rust protects it from further corrosion.

Pages 162 and 163

The building in Central Park just below the Reservoir is the Metropolitan Museum of Art on Fifth Avenue at 82nd Street, the largest art museum in the western hemisphere, and growing. The tall tower on the Hudson River above the end of the Park is Riverside Church at 121st Street. The domed structure immediately to its right is Columbia University and the two domes to its left are part of the Cathedral of Saint John The Divine.

Pages 164 and 165

Of all the things the hand of man has placed on the island of Manhattan, the 840 acres of Central Park is still the most wonderful. The first tree was planted in 1858. By 1873, five million vines, trees and shrubs were planted. In the beginning there were 42 species of trees growing in Manhattan. When it opened, Central Park had more than 600, all thriving and happy to have become Manhattanites.

Pages 166 and 167

The boats that take visitors on pilgrimages to the Statue of Liberty sail in all kinds of weather whenever Liberty Island is open to the public. The half-hour boat ride is an impressive part of the experience.

Page 168

Excavations for the six buildings of the World Trade Center produced more than 23 acres of landfill in the Hudson River. It wasn't wasted. By the end of 1986, it will be home to more than 45,000 people, many of whom are already at home here in Battery Park City. A lot of them won't have far to go to work when the World Financial Center becomes home to such corporate giants as American Express.